AF605613

I BELIEVE IN YOU

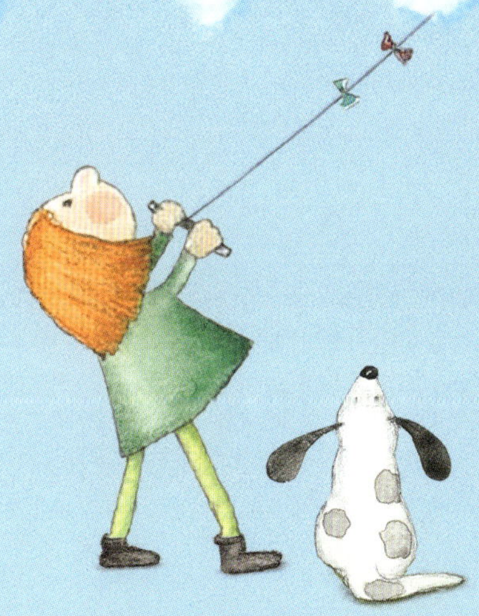

DANI COLVIN

Blair was feeling blue.

Not blue like the sky
or a swimming pool
or the world's biggest whale.
Those are nice, **sparkly** blues.

No, Blair was a **gloomy** blue.

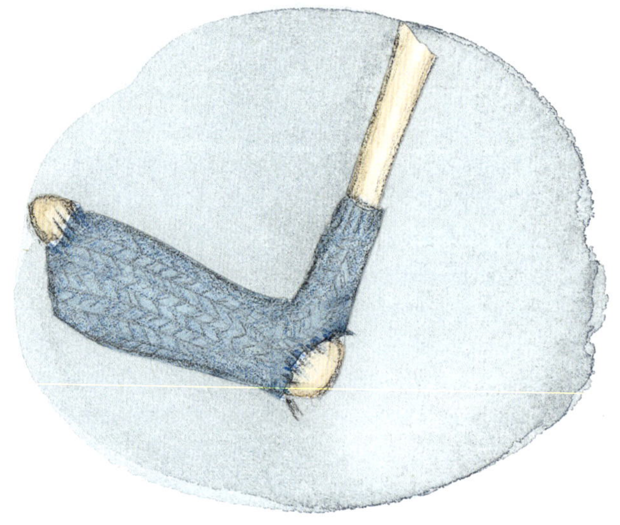

Blue like a holey sock
on a winter's day,

like a messy ink splodge
on a clean page,

like a tiny boat lost
on a vast ocean . . .

like all those feelings rolled into a great big,
heavy, sighing thing, squishing the air out of Blair.

Luckily, Grandpa was waiting with a **warm hug** and a **hot chocolate**, as he always was when he was needed most.

'I've got something important to tell you,'
he said gently, 'so listen up, my darling bear.'

The world can be a tricky place
and you sometimes wonder why
it seems to bite you on the bottom
or poke you in the eye.

You feel life's turned against you
and you just can't get things right.

You feel powerless and lonely
and it's hard to find some light.

But I've got news for you, oh yes,
I'll set the record straight.
I think that you're **spectacular!**
I think that you are **great!**

You fear you aren't ... or won't ... or can't ...
but darling, that's not true.

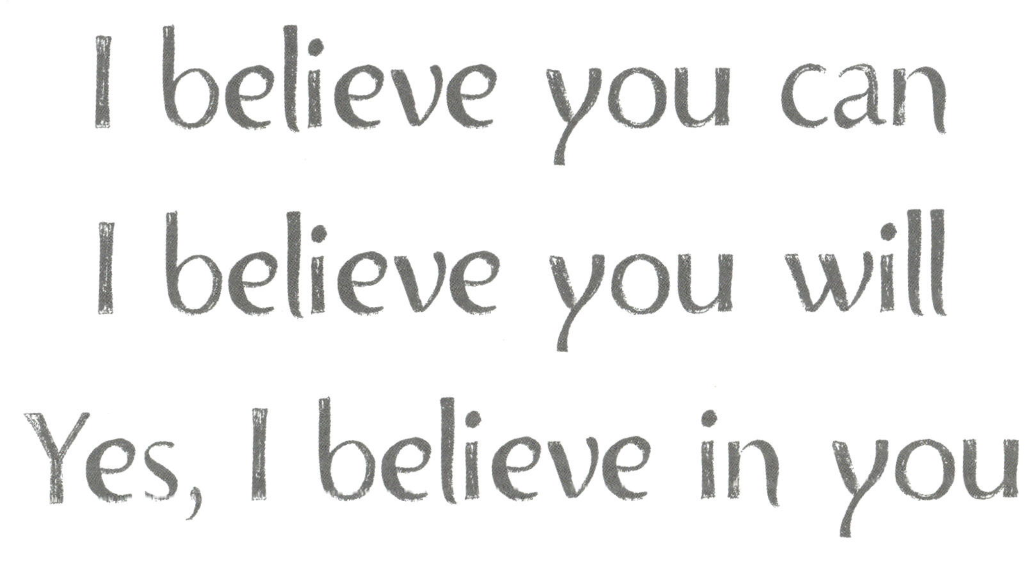

You have **courage** in abundance
like a lion in your heart.

You're important and you matter –
you are kind are strong and smart.

The tiny voice inside your head
may tell you
you can't do it.
Just don't believe a word it says
and please don't listen to it.

But hear me when I tell you
because every word is true:

Mistakes are part of life
and everybody makes them.

They're how we learn for next time
so don't worry, just embrace them.

Those hiccups show you tried
and put in effort, thought and care.
They show at least that you showed up
and show you dared to dare.

The going might be hard sometimes ...
the path might get quite rough.
You'll sometimes think of giving up
but you're made of sterner stuff.

And I'll lovingly remind you
when you've forgotten that it's true ...

In time you'll learn to trust more
in your strength and in your power.
To run the longer race
and to endure the darkest hour.

So dream your dreams!
Go chase them boldly, one step at a time.
I'll be so proud to see you reach them,
prouder still to watch you climb.

And tell yourself these words, whenever doubt creeps in anew …

"I believe I can,

I believe I will"

so YOU believe in YOU!

Well, as you might have guessed, Grandpa's words helped.
The gloomy blue began to shrink and shrink.
Finally, it was so tiny, it simply floated off into the distance.
And bit by bit, other colours crept into Blair's heart –

First, came a warm,
tingly yellow . . .

then **fluttery** orange . . .

fizzy red . . .

sproingy green . . .

and even **sparkly** blue.

Like the sky

or a swimming pool . . .

or the world's
biggest
whale.

To my dad and my beautiful boys. Always.

I Believe in You
first published in 2025
by Walker Books Australia Pty Ltd
Gadigal and Wangal Country
Locked Bag 22, Newtown
NSW 2042 Australia
www.walkerbooks.com.au

Walker Books Australia acknowledges the Traditional Owners of the country on which we work, the Gadigal and Wangal peoples of the Eora Nation, and recognises their continuing connection to the land, waters and culture. We pay our respect to their Elders past and present.

A catalogue record for this book is available from the National Library of Australia

ISBN: 978 1 760656 13 3

The illustrations for this book were created with watercolour, pencil and collage
Typeset in Boudoir Bold
Printed and bound in China
EU Authorized Representative: HackettFlynn Ltd, 36 Cloch Choirneal, Balrothery, Co. Dublin, K32 C942, Ireland. EU@walkerpublishinggroup.com

10 9 8 7 6 5 4 3 2 1